Motes at Play in the Halls of Light

Motes at Play in the Halls of Light

Poems by

Devon Balwit

Kelsay Books

© 2017 Devon Balwit. All rights reserved. This material may not be reproduced in any form, published, reprinted, recorded, performed, broadcast, rewritten or redistributed without the explicit permission of Devon Balwit. All such actions are strictly prohibited by law.

Cover photograph "Said" © Dirk Bakker 1994

ISBN: 13-978-1-947465-33-6

Kelsay Books
Aldrich Press
www.kelsaybooks.com

*To my husband, Fritz, who has surrounded me with many lifetimes
of inspiration and to my children, Xander, Avital, and Theo,
who have been far more patient with my muse
than any mother could expect.*

Acknowledgments

Non-Binary Review: A Modest Proposal
Traveling Uterus: A Stubborn Country
Shantih: A Tented Space against Wind
In a Woman's Voice: A Woman Scorned
Audiophile Audition: An ingenious jesting with art
Jenny: At the Flower Market
Trailhead Magazine: Bishop's Lie
Red Earth Review: Elgar, Listening
Smeuse: Envy
Red Paint Hill: Evolutionary
The Cincinnati Review: Exhumed
How the Blessed Travel: Fleeting
3 Elements: Gauntlet
Tule Review: Gratitude
Dying Dahlia Review: Hive Sisters
Muse/A Journal: In Anticipation Of
Former People: In the Ring
Minute: Lapidary
Black Lawrence Press: A Collaborative Anthology: Letting Bones Speak
Free State Review: Metamorphosis
Of Painted Words: Motes at Play in the Halls of Light
Malevolent Soap: Naked
Emrys Journal: Naked Mary
Brave New Word: Night Stadium
Aeolian Harp Anthology: Nightly
DMQ: No Elegy
Calamus: No Knowledge without Pain
Pacifica: One with Borders Forever Shifting
Fire Poetry: Painter to the Moon
All the Sins: Peroration
Solidago: Precisely
Carolina Quarterly: Privy to Secrets, Punch Drunk

Visual Verse: Prodigal
Unlikely Stories Mark V: Refugees
Dream Fever Magazine: Returning to Petroglyphs
Aeolian Harp Anthology: Seeing Where We Are Led
The Ekphrastic Review: Self-Portraits
Peacock Journal (*): Interruptions & Sitting on the Wall
Aeolian Harp Anthology: The Doula Says Push to the Crowning
Poets Reading the News: The Thin Line
Anti-Heroin Chic: The Triumph of Mediocrity
Infinity's Kitchen: Ushering in the Apocalypse
Poetry Pacific: What Floats
Rat's Ass Review: What Wouldn't You Give in Return

(*) Also published in the chapbook "How the Blessed Travel" (Maverick Duck Press)

Contents

Dieu crée l'Homme	15
Gauntlet	16
What Wouldn't You Give in Return?	17
Evolutionary	18
Prodigal	19
Exhumed	20
White Noise	21
Motes at Play in the Halls of Light	23
Sleight of Hand	24
Envy	25
At the Flower Market	26
Homo Ludens	27
We Take Up Our Instruments	28
Black Sienna: A Rorschach	29
Lapidary	30
No Elegy	31
Naked	32
In Anticipation Of	33
Self-Portraits	34
"An Ingenious Jesting with Art"	35
What Floats	36
A Stubborn Country	37
Dear Swarm,	38
A Woman Scorned	39
Cool	40
Naked Mary	41
A Trick of Light	42
At this Very Moment	43
Metamorphosis	45
Zambezia, Zambezia	46
Sitting on the Wall	47
Restraint	48

Spectacle	49
Punch Drunk	50
Briefly	51
Interruption	52
Night Stadium	53
Elgar, Listening	54
No Knowledge without Pain	55
The Thin Line	57
Ushering in the Apocalypse: Parabolic Poem ($x2 + 1$)	59
The Triumph of Mediocrity	61
Privy to Secrets	62
Nightly	63
A Modest Proposal	64
Letting Bones Speak	65
A Tented Space against Wind	66
Seeing Where We Are Led	67
On Falling in Love at 54	69
Dear Prick, Priapic	71
Peroration	72
Precisely	73
Painter to the Moon	74
Refugees	75
The Doula Says Push to the Crowning	76
Epilogue	77

About the Author

Dieu crée l'Homme

after Marc Chagall

Chagall has God's angel running like a criminal
        after being handed man,

fleeing like a smash and grab through darkness lit
        by G(יהוה)d's eye, solitary,

chased by all the fiends of hell, perhaps trying
        to outrun the future, the wars

hard on each other's heels, the lynch mobs
        clamoring, knowing already

what his dreaming burden would get up to.
        Adam sleeps through the commotion,

fully-formed, penis small and harmless as a boy's,
        the angel's wing like a pillow

cushioning the frantic footfalls. Eve exists only
        in the shadow of Adam's cupped hand.

The ray of light emanating from the Divine
        looks very like a prod, ensuring

the angel can stagger in one direction only—
        away.

Gauntlet

From the walls of Lascaux, Chauvet, Cueva de la Araña
a glaze of ochre threads us to the past, to human thinking

and doing. There, by candle flicker, artists set bison
to pound turf, released predatory cats, handed bow

to hunter, smoking torch to honey gatherer. They spread
their own hands against the dark wall of time and blew

pigment, outlining deft fingers. They made worship
visible, the small yearning for great comfort. Eight, ten

thousand years later, their voices still murmur, still
speak of kinship. Their craft echoes a challenge,

and I wonder, millennia hence, if our pixels will answer.
Power out, what have we made that will last?

What Wouldn't You Give in Return?

*I would give all metaphors
in return for one word
drawn out of my breast like a rib*
 —Zbigniew Herbert

Sentimentality: not jam on the bread, but jam on the face,
he said. If only it were so easy to keep the jam where

it belongs. You plunge your hand into rushing water
hoping for an agate, but sometimes, you just get a stone.

You know you should let the stone stay a stone if that's
what it wants, but still you squeeze, demanding a word.

The word should be cut from your breast like a rib, and set
free to organize its half of Eden, but you can't help interfering,

renaming the animals and replanting trees where you think
they should go. No wonder you end up naked and sticky,

the snake flicking its long tongue in satisfaction at how it has
tricked you once again into cliché. Now you will be cast out

to wander and bring forth in pain. Fear not, this you can use.
The trick is to make your pain your own and no one else's,

the jam the bread's and no one else's, the rib the rib's and no
one else's. Skip the stone and go right to the heart of the matter,

the incision, the reaching into yourself, the hole where you are now
incomplete, the infinity which you can pack into your nothingness.

Evolutionary

Perhaps the full moon routed sleep,
or the front-page photograph on my lawn
of mouse paw & fish fin, Hoxa 13 markers
glowing a green trail back 430 million years
to when all of us paddled the same pond,

back to before we tinkered with genes,
crafting mice with long leg bones but no arms
or fish to spin finless, back to before
we interfered with the creatures, stripping them
of skin & habitat, before we made them sit up

& beg or swim circles, the moon's flat disc
offering no commentary as it spotlights
our progress from cave painting to screen,
from spear point to gunfire. Only we humans
can say *enough*, or say nothing, bank our roads

this way or that. A jet grumbles in the night sky,
a fan whirs. I await bird song as a supplicant
the host, promising to make something of myself,
while elsewhere floodwaters recede on silt,
brushfires ash, a child walks the long road

for water. The moon covers itself in branches
as the sky greys enough to see the newspaper
& its ephemera awaiting compost, their journey
back to the vegetal, together with the ancestors
swimming in me as I set oar to current

Prodigal

All those years you spent hard after love
forgetting your own face, cleaved down

to heartwood, the reflective pools of your
own eyes spilling clouds. Now you are back,

door slamming behind you, duffle bulked
in the hall. Throw your arms around

your shoulders, congratulatory. Invite all
who know you, kill the fatted calf, raise a stink

of charred fat to god's nose. While everyone
is still gorging, hard in their cups, slip away

to the most secret of beds. There, lip to lip,
rediscover the one who loves you best.

Exhumed

With every turn of the winch, the alabaster corpses rise,
torsos graceful, water streaming from chiseled eyes,
reaching arms, broken off at the wrists.

How the sun hurtles, no matter how gently we are exhumed.
The shock of it crumbles our edges, drops bits of us earthward
to be lost among pebbles.

You the living, fingers interlaced, imagine you will stay whole.
Yet, someday, fragments of your caress will adorn a small pedestal
among all the others, *circa* and date on a yellowing tag.

Help me find my own remains, a still-living infant pulled from
rubble. Set me to suckle at a stranger's breast, plaster dusting
our tear-streaked cheeks.

White Noise

after Joseph Brodsky

The most definitive feature of antiquity
    is our absence.

Take the long view in either direction,
    and we disappear,

and so, the selfies. *Marble negates us*
    particularly well...

Colorless, sometimes limbless, most certainly
    mute. Mute

we are not. What a horror, the nothing
    behind and before,

thus, the overfilling of the moment,
    the flood of words,

the asking *Who is there? Who is listening?*
    the fascination

with each other's bottoms, the anus sniffing.
    Time is no jigsaw puzzle,

because it is made up of perishing pieces.
    No more. Leave

a large enough digital footprint,
    and we never die.

Pitying the blank busts, we coopt them,
    certain their subjects

would have it so, the hunger for more
    the original hunger.

Motes at Play in the Halls of Light

We always glance slantwise at beauty, turning
to it our Janus-faced wonderment and envy,

wanting to be of and in the light but dragged
downwards by cracked-clay heaviness, a base

that can only hold the glowing filament, so easily
jarred to breaking. See the eyes, shadow-traced,

refracted into panes? Each holds the painter's
palette, the aperture, the pen—missals to summon

the muse, nets to trawl for awe. We must catch
the spilling while we're quick. We won't be long.

Sleight of Hand

after Joan Miró

The artist has saddled his work with a title to lead us
    astray, like a killdeer flopping in the grass

or a magician, who makes us look elsewhere while
    a mother calls for a lost child, not lost,

only hiding. He distracts the eye, ever-scanning
    for things too bright for camouflage,

the lacewings whose blood brims a poison even the hungry
    can't stomach. Following his finger,

we miss the line we mustn't cross, lush and sere
    kept at arm's length. We turn away

from the white-rimmed startle, from the secret space
    where a stranger plies puppet-clad hands.

Envy

> *My heart in hiding / Stirred for a bird, —the achieve of; the mastery of the thing!*
>
> —Gerard Manley Hopkins

And what wouldn't I, chair-bound, tethered, give
to rise, wheel, lift myself above concerns and
pettiness, entrust myself to gust and updraft, look
down on humankind become mouse-like in their
burrows, furrowed brow smoothing, heeding only
current and breeze, released from those grounded,
founding joy on wingturn, banked pinions alone,
the only gold, sun-dappled flap and eye-glare,
hunting small scurryings, whirring wings pulled
abruptly in to arrow down to blood reward, the
hot meat of the sought picked from bone, feeding
future flight, nothing wasted, nothing mourned.

At the Flower Market

for Xander

To get there, I ride the slipstream of eighteen-wheelers,
past the railyard and the docks to where knowing resides

not just in the head but in the fingertips stripping dead blooms,
dead leaves, pressing soil to the knuckle to gauge how deep

a drink, how dry a drought, how long since stems rooted in dirt.
Here beauty bides its time, sunflowers bundled and netted

in the cold room, geraniums, roses, and ranunculus pressed,
like with like, while, elsewhere, beneath warming lamps,

the lush mouths of dancing ladies and cymbidiums await occasion.
The bit players texture pallets, fern, bells of Ireland, curly willow,

holding still as trained eyes picture them lifting prima donnas
on a future stage. The armature for every rite stock steel shelves,

in a spectrum from birth to mourning: bowers for brides, balloons
for babies, easels for the dead, cards ready for congratulation

or condolence. The air wafts resinous and floral, set to thicken
to full fragrance once warm. I take everything in, wishing

I had reason to linger, that my forbears hadn't abandoned the
field for the cubicle, trading one cultivation for quite another.

Homo Ludens

A painting is not a structure of colors and lines, but an animal,
a night, a cry, a man, or all of these together
—Constant Nieuwenhuys

Oh, wat een ding is man, (says the canvas beneath
the artist's brush), his parts unfurling like birdsong,

or reassembling from bits at the toybox bottom.
He staggers about the agora, neck swiveling,

clacking placards, the wagonwheels of his hip
joints turning, a tossing of color from one

to the next, the yarn-tuft hair, womb-spooled.
Great and small warp fast, shuttles dance.

He holds his pose, ironic, before the stage curtain,
meeting, head-on, the shaft that is either a spear

or a ray of light. *Man, een ding is, een gekke ding*
(says the long-suffering canvas, touched and re-

touched), yet wherever he gathers, a city shakes
itself, cymbals after a cesura, a shuddering ovation.

We Take Up Our Instruments

Dawn clashes window-glass,
as the city readies its ghosts.

We baton-tap from dreams, up
tempo, lento, those who rest.

A man spins at the bus stop.
A woman pads the bridges barefoot.

Beneath tarps, industry,
the unhoused wringing life

from the margins. Held
at the wrist, a child twists,

taking it all in, staring, big-eyed
at a woman with a dog

in her tote-bag, lipstick smile
wandering down a cheek.

Buskers ready strings.
The blue toothed colloquize air.

Soon, comes the full din,
the huff of brakes, the trains'

clakketa, theme and variation,
room for the unexpected.

Black Sienna: A Rorschach

after Franz Kline

Within you, a splotch, a smear knotted
    just beneath the breastbone.

You unfold it into a black swan,
    a small man in a beret hunched

before an easel. Back and forth across
    your eyelids, the treads

of a tank press the dead deep into no-
    man's land. With a sinking and

a sucking, a panther gnaws, head thrust
    between split ribs. You are

an oyster, gutted by a shucker's knife,
    a shadowy shelf fungus.

Tilt your head, even a fraction, and
    your smudge lies, differently.

Lapidary

The overflow from the roof gutters spatters
the sidewalks murky

before pooling in the streets for passing cars
to raise in chill spray.

At work, our breakroom talk
is about abstinence—

no caffeine, no alcohol—as if by refusing,
we could become immortal.

The homeless have abandoned the sodden park
for the foyer,

but each time they lay down, they are made
to rise again, company policy

allowing bodies upright, but not prone.
This isn't a good city,

one repeats, hauling herself up. The security guard
pats her shoulder

and asks where she'd rather be. A coworker mentions
she's just learned the word

lapidary, and I wonder how she managed
for thirty-one years with no way

to describe our collisions, the slurry of days
that tumbles us smooth.

No Elegy

it's early
the dead still
unnamed
harm
at its apogee
screams
quiet
in throats
the lion and the gazelle
frozen
in the tall grass
grief
embryonic
fingers
lifted
over keys
here
nothing
has happened
heads
nestle in pillows
still attached
to necks
here
there is
nothing
yet
to grieve

Naked

The melting snow has returned the world
like a water-dipped cat, thin beneath its fur.
Here is a pen dropped in the storm. There
a pothole, edges crumbling. After so much
white, the colors clamor, noisy as children
when the school doors open. Along the road,
melting heaps wear jagged in rain, dolmens
to forgotten rites. Fractured branches attest
to what was lost, the weight of silence,
the laziness of hours. I peel back skin and
peel back skin upon ever-smaller replicas.
I remain a wingless grub. Instigating, a
young boy smashes his own chest with a
handful of ice. I touch a tiny mound nestled
among garden-roots, then drag cool fingers
across my cheeks, claiming my own scars.

In Anticipation Of

after Cristina Troufa

I hold a glass to the ear of your concern,
amplifying the dark throb

till all of me tingles as I do on the crest
of orgasm.

Soon you will shatter against me in a spray
of salt and broken things

before sucking back into the swell to gather
once again.

The sound of you penetrates, the tremor
of invisible faults.

Imprudent, I have prepared nothing and
will suffer,

my empty hands beseeching from the frame.
That time is not yet.

For now, I press myself to you, so concentrated
you might be sleeping.

Self-Portraits

Twenty times the artist revisited the wreckage of his face
the way I do certain photographs—the dead stacked like
cordwood at Buchenwald, the naked girl running from
napalm at Trang Bang, the suited man plummeting on 9/11.
These people knew death first hand, were its messengers.
Like Terence, Albright claims through his blasted faces:
Homo sum, humani nihil a me alienum puto. "Nothing
human is alien to me—even if I have become an alien
to myself." I bow to Albright's bravery. I stagger
when I face my corruption in the mirror—my waist giving
out like rotten elastic, my skin creping, my once thick hair
a razed field. Each of his portraits catalogues the horror anew—
age spots, puffiness, wrinkles, balding, fear, rheumy eyes.
Each bellows: I am staring down the worst of it and still,
Homo Faber, I create. In a world that worships youth,
what is more gruesome than an old woman—unsexed,
blown? Yet, I would revisit my demise in endless variation,
even as he did until his final days, reduced and reduced
until all that remained were his fierce eyes. Perhaps, like God,
I will distill to a single word, my own *yod-hey-vav-hey*.

"An Ingenious Jesting with Art"

was what Scarlatti called his compositions,
555 of them, no two alike, all disobedient

to the rules of music, inviting peasant
dances and roughhousing into halls of gilt

and inlay, all done while thumbing his nose
at Mr. Oratorio, Mr. Opera—his father—

All tumbled into the world from a man
no longer young. With luck, rejection,

the lapidary roil of hurt, polishes dazzling.
Listen to their lilt, fingers dappling keys

like wind or rain the surface of a lake,
a shaking loose of light. Are his japes aimed at

or made from artistry, an ingenious declaration?
Hands rush to ripple, slow, and rest,

releasing a beauty close to anguish, what a poet called
"a hail of glistening pearls, bubbles

of watery beauty." Downriver, we patter and break
with their sparkle, refracting bright beams.

What Floats

It's the time of year
        when small ants

invade the cupboards,
        marching from outside

in files as if underscoring
        the encroaching weather.

All night, rain
        burbles in the gutters,

rustling as it falls
        with TV static.

I expect to step from bed
        into knee-deep water,

but the only pool
        is in my head,

a catchment of decades,
        ever-rising.

Some days, I fish out
        the dead, others,

whatever floats
        from watery darkness,

wrung from the world
        by its turning.

A Stubborn Country

The first thing I pack and the last I unpack
is always myself, this thing that I wear and
wring, then dry on a door handle, ever more
wrinkled, never right for the occasion.

Caelum non animum mutant qui trans mare currunt—
I sling myself over my shoulders to squares
and cathedrals, cafes and alleyways, project myself
onto the locals going about their business:

crossing roads with no lights, bartering, balancing
baskets and babies, or wearing elegantly what I
would look clownish in. I wonder how crazy
I would be here, who my friends would be,

what my conveyance and who my lover, what my
job and what my view. I take no photos, for my
inner voice puts a foot down, calling it intrusive;
What I want to keep, I'll have to remember.

After I return, I wonder if I ever went, so clogged
is my head with myself, so loud my own
clarion. I like to think I've crossed borders,
but I remain—a stubborn country of one.

Dear Swarm,

Doubtful you remember me from back then, skirting
the margins, hunching my brightness into shadows.

In those days, I tucked my head like a letter flap,
protecting the heart of me. You wanted me to fear you

always, never knowing where you lurked, from where
you'd spring. You delighted in each fall, each shamefaced

splay, plucked my wings one by one, then plucked
the regrowing nubs. I know now what it was—boredom,

fear—your own self unfurling too nakedly. Better to
bloody the goat, to deflect wrath and feel saved. Were I

vengeful, I'd wish your children me and you watching.
I am not. All I want is this moment of your time.

Love,
That Girl

A Woman Scorned

Nowhere now safe for you. If I could train
the ground itself to flinch at your step,

you would plummet to magma. The wind
would slap at you, dry leaves flensing.

Instead, I've recruited the small things,
the wire walkers, the nut gatherers.

Their chittering coded, alerting
the canopy. You with your new love

on a picnic blanket. Hitchcockian,
they come in phalanx, tails lifted like

pennants. Think of me with each bite,
a rancor that leaves you faceless.

Cool

after Hodaka Yoshida

All blue elegance, I sip the city's
champagne flute, let sweaty streets

effervesce before they knock
against my lids to be let in. I am

the diminished chord, the muted
brass, the drummer's light brush.

Slip your arms around my hips,
and you must wait. Only after

my last exhale, applause fading,
will I lead you to bed. There,

I am lamp-glow between slats,
the siren's Doppler, approaching

and receding. When I tell you go,
don't linger. Months from now,

don't follow me. I know these streets
better than you, each vanishing point.

Naked Mary

after Otto Dix

Naked Mary has an ass like a walrus,
the chair her beach, cheeks sunning

themselves by lantern light. If she catches
you staring, she laughs. *Give 'em a slap;*

they won't bite, she invites, and if you do,
she likes you better for it. Beneath her knees,

pink garters ruffle, twin schoolgirls who
have somehow lost their way and cling,

awaiting rescue. No matter how tired her feet,
her heels stay on. *At the end of the night,*

each inch is an extra dollar, she rasps. Mary
would know, cigarette all but ash in its holder.

She was my first and always satisfies. Better
than old marrieds, we fuck and laugh, never

mistaking what we do for love, the
bald fact of bills left on the nightstand.

A Trick of Light

At such an hour, our shadows hunger
    to abandon us.

Barely tethered by toe tips, they work
    to escape hindering.

Their cheeks offer blankness, secrets
    tucked, haughty,

into forbidding grey. But the time
    always comes to reconcile:

no apology,
    no confession.

At this Very Moment

within the synapses of your brain, leaves
 are fueling thoughts of leaves, sunlight

turns sugar through alchemy. You play
 and replay cows

sitting in the lap of the farmer. Elephants
 gently stroke a tourist's face,

dogs' nuzzle their masters' necks, even a chicken
 races to greet a man,

a fish swims into an open palm. Canyons, copses,
 the horizon line,

all meet you halfway, absorbing you so your ego
 might rest a moment.

Always in a frenzy of dismemberment, you need
 felling, as with a maul,

to drop and be still. Whales, you learn,
 aerate the ocean, plunging

fathoms-deep. Their shit manures the waters;
 in its wake, krill blooms.

You know this matters only to a few, soon not at all,
 the whole marvel darkening

to *once was*. Already, you count fewer butterflies,
    fewer birds. Only the heartiest

join the dawn chorus—the crows and seagulls,
    cagey adaptors. You think thoughts

conjured by waving branches. All give way
    to streets that will one day empty.

title quote by Hope Jahren

Metamorphosis

after Joan Miró

At the center, a busy shadow, pants down
around its ankles. Or perhaps, anchored
on booted feet, half an angel, one wing

gone. There, too, an elephant rests,
hands on hips, a frowny sort of thing,
trunk like a wagging finger, eye, a tit.

Both are busy, the shadow emptying soot
from pocket-deeps, the elephant scrubbing
clean. Nemeses, they do and undo,

counterweights of a mighty clock that
bongs when it pleases. I dizzy myself
squinting between the lines, trying

to name tools and intentions. Just
as my mouth rounds for the *aha*, someone
asks, *and what of the butterflies?*

Zambezia, Zambezia

after Wifredo Lam

What we don't know, we call Zambia,
exaggerating darkness, seeing juju in each

bent twig and fallen feather, naming
its spirits resentful and malevolent.

We demand cheetah pelts and feathered
crowns, bare-breasted women with babies

strapped to their backs, not jeans
and Adidas. Our Zambezi writhes

in its banks, does not sluggishly shoulder
motorboats. We resent the encroachment

of the global, even as the Zambians
themselves gladly fire up loud generators,

lighting the night and watching Game
of Thrones while chatting on mobiles.

We prefer the Zambia of steatopygian shadows,
drummers, witch doctors, and conical huts,

telling its natives they know nothing
at all about themselves and should leave

their exposition to those more passionate—
us, to whom Zambezia whispers.

Sitting on the Wall

her chest opens to waxwings, to the wind
    that sounds her, unstopped.

Holding her own hand, she shuts eyes
    on dusk's peony flush,

her chignon snugging its weight of want
    to her nape,

a single strand slipped to ripple alongside
    the blown seeds lazing ever farther

as they sink. She watches one till it disappears
    between blades,

then stands, her hands falling to her hips,
    her hips falling

into the rhythm of steps. Somewhere, an ear
    returns her echo.

Restraint

after Wassily Kandinsky

The furnace beckons with its molten eye.
I am tempted to topple, ready to burn.

Instead, I blink complementary colors,
reach for a brush not the bellows, standing

near but not in the crucible. Every day,
compelled by red-hot, I toy with immolation,

but, in the end, call ruddy reflection
close enough. I work its palette of blue

and tan, trying to make the almost dance.
Drawing the assay away from the coals,

I bang against what has come before,
learning which blows shake to marrow.

Spectacle

after Wassily Kandinsky

The circus has claimed the cellular membrane,
    a busker's harp

bewitching a dancing horse, centrioles piping
    for fan-dancers,

the beguiling moon. Clownish golgi bodies
    dodge mitochondria

as spring bulbs part granular soil. Take it all in,
    but make way

for the barkers impatient for shills.
    Feel no shame

in joining their number. Gawk at the bearded
    lady, the two-headed boy.

Overhead, the sky stoops, stars spilling
    from dark pockets,

the night throbbing with the frenzy of zipping
    and unzipping.

Punch Drunk

after Kurt Schwitters

Sometimes you are a small butterfly, willfully in the wrong
painting, an Oregon silverspot, let's say, or a painted lady,

delicately poised on a Basquiat or Schwitters, the colors
screaming all around, shapes closing in, but you, choosing

to remain, perverse, wings opening and closing, having decided
to throw off genres, to say to hell with critics. You rest

your Dutch Master realism smack dab amidst chaos, making
the whole jingle-jangle before it resettles, you the focal point,

all those angry angles grinding their teeth, unseen wind
shivering your scales, you, punch drunk with sweetness.

Briefly

This in gratitude for dawn, guarding the gates of night,
beheading any escapees, and for the morning chorus drowning
out the three a.m. voices, for the downshifting of eighteen-
wheelers, the metal clang, the cocks' crow—sweet—
for the opalescence soothing midnight's acidity,
repinking it like healthy tissue, for the ability to rise
and go about my business, ordinary, and not a revenant,
for the boat-tailed grackles in their loopy flight,
hauling me by sheer ridiculousness from my well,
for cirrus clouds, suggesting, like a first sketch, space
and volume. The day will condense, of course, funneling
again to the hours of battle, but for now, dawn absolves me.

Interruption

The deer cross the marsh left to right,
    spattering reflected sky.

Hooves stir storm circles from clouds.
    Reeds stipple

like flocking on Chinese silk, the landscape
    worn by the season.

Three follow one in front, a fletched
    arrow arced

towards evening when bodies curl close.
    The plash of hooves

defies the hunter, each shy enough this day
    to remain quick.

After their passing, gravity returns the water
    to firmament.

Night Stadium

*Thank you for sending poems. You have obvious skill,
but none of these quite convinces me of its urgency,
if you know what I mean.*

after Wassily Kandinsky

Stacked hurdles spike a palisade. Even
with enough urgency, I cannot clear
them, or I'll be skewered, food
for shrikes. The bare bleachers offer

no encouragement, nor the sand pits,
naked without jumpers. *Home*,
the scoreboard lies, *Visitors*, devoid of
welcome. The score remains zero / zero.

With enough urgency, guests become
family, entering the fray. Without it,
there's no contest; no one stumbles
or mounts the podium. Javelin and

discus sulk in their racks. Why the long
face? Why the disorder? *That's why
we need passion*, coach bellows. *Drop
and give me twenty*. Without urgency,

it'll be twenty more. I push off against
the starting blocks, run the long laps
round, chasing my shadow as it
shapeshifts beneath floodlights.

Without urgency, the flag droops,
helmet crests hang, ornamental.
The eyes of history are upon me. I
picture the tape as I hurtle through.

Elgar, Listening

*In 1923, at the age of sixty-six, composer Edward Elgar
took a voyage to Brazil, journeying up the Amazon to Manaus.
Almost nothing is known of his trip.*

He leans over the steamship stern, captivated
by passing trogons, howler monkeys, butterflies

waving like ladies' scarves. Behind him, his work
dissipates in the boat's wake, swirling into eddies.

Heedless of any baton, fish plash the river's surface,
a seedpod plunges like a struck drum, insects hum,

sailors curse and call, basso profondo, while a woman
laughs in the upper registers. He does not know

what to make of it, how to carry it back. For
sixty-six years, he moved in one direction,

towards acclaim, security, only to open its door
on an empty room. There, he strained for a theme.

Here, he finds too many—the tangle of lianas, humidity,
rot, rain pelting the river in sheets. Does he have

the courage to return and do nothing, see what
germinates, brave his wife's anxious ghost as he sits

before silent staves, ears cocked to the not yet? Fingers
tapping the splintered rail, he hears in his pulse

the laboring of great paddles, feels himself
driven, born inexorably away.

No Knowledge without Pain

Humboldt puzzled over electricity.
When a farmer and his wife were struck

by lightning, he anatomized their corpses,
noting leg bones pierced as if by shotgun pellets,

the charred genitalia. Leaning over a frog
pinned to his dissection table, nerves

delicately wired, the moisture in his breath
caused the leg to jerk. He felt a very god,

breathing life into brute matter.
In the Venezuelan Llanos, he delighted

at ponds of Gymnotiformes—electric eels—
but how to catch the 800 volts of them

without self-harm? Solicitous locals
rounded up wild horses, sent them

to churn murk and awaken the sleepers.
Safe on shore, Humboldt and companions

watched the jolted whinnying, the frantic
trampling as equines drowned

beneath desperate hooves. How satisfying
the interplay of such wild forces.

Back in his tent, Humboldt shocked
himself, feet in water and on dry ground,

attaching electrodes, bits of wax, palm
and wet clay to these clamped creatures—

horse, eel, land, man surging in wonderment:
no knowledge without its attendant pain.

The Thin Line

The pub ambiance burnishes the ice
melting in our glasses as you tell me
of people, this very week, here and

elsewhere, cutting the noses and ears
off living dogs. I want to slap you
for opening the door to pain, for

letting it pad in, bleeding, trailing
theodicy behind, for reminding me
that as I sit here, sipping house red,

in another house, the red is of a
different kind, a blunt force trauma
to the soul, a damage that doesn't

heal but festers. You insist it is so,
obligating me to look, for how
can I write what I can't imagine?

Who takes a selfie flaunting the ears
of a dog above the maimed animal?
My cruelties are not of the same order,

I insist, and they are not, but what
makes similar hands hunger for harm?
Look at a graphic of a geological clock,

the thin sliver of human history,
the billions of years in which we
made no headline news, nestled in

our forebears, the tiniest of shrews.
Then think of the thin needle of fate
quivering before it set us down where

it did in the body it did, cloaking our
inner machinery with pigmented skin,
or giving us a womb, or making us draw

our first breath with the muezzin's cry,
in a gated community, a tent, a tenement,
with guardians loving or brutal. That

improbable line set some up to be holding
the knife and others fearful of it, set me up
to be looking at you, aghast at your tainting

my evening with suffering. The night is no
longer for sleeping, instead it becomes an
interrogation, of those men lifting soft ears,

of me, turning away, of what horror requires
of me. You opened the door; I want to slap you.
My hands lift. You are gone. I set them here.

Ushering in the Apocalypse: Parabolic Poem $(x^2 + 1)$

I.
The gutters overflow, ice blocking the
drainpipes. We watch the
flood, but
do
nothing.
Easier to mourn
the damp and wax nostalgic for what was.

II.
Slap me if I make you nervous. I won't
hold it against you.
I would
slap
me, too,
if our roles reversed.
I accept what is written in the stars.

III.
In the movies, Lady Liberty's torch
or the rotting flag
in the
House
Chamber
reveals us to be
on Earth. We need similar markers now.

IV.
Tell me I will awaken like Sleeping
Beauty from a dream.
I will
look
up at
you, lips still tingling,
then rise to clear away dust and cobwebs.

The Triumph of Mediocrity

Sometimes, half-assed is the best you can do,
the pot half-cleaned, the fence propped, the
buckling floor pressed flat with books. You
learn to dial down want.

You go to work, but your mind toggles
elsewhere. You stare through your cubicle
at an invisible horizon, the answers you give
do not bear scrutiny.

Back home, you and your one-time-love
share a domicile the way strangers do
an elevator, each taking a quadrant,
careful not to crowd.

Even your insomnia falls short, the same
fears recycled until, like a much-read letter,
they split at the seams, leaving you casting
about for a reason to wander.

You give thanks for tepidity, knowing the great
draw the scythe. Better to go camouflaged
like a bird dropping, able to rise once
the raptors have flown.

Privy to Secrets

He is irascible. I am erased. The light fixture hanging
in the almost-blackness like a bat. A sideways staring

at a half-open drawer, familiar shot elastic out-peeking.
He is livid. I am ludic. The angrier he gets, the more

I laugh. An inappropriate response, but in my own
defense, are we not comic in rage (so long as our hands

are weaponless)? Caveats flutter about me the way
butterflies once did in my youth. Now, they are

gone. One species after another, settling itself to sleep
in the loving brushstrokes of extinction. I bite my lip,

wring my hands, counting seconds until the next thing.
He is pedantic. I am pudic. Holding my opinions

close to my chest, tearing them small and swallowing.
Blood flares in cheeky braziers. I am a quark, a muon.

Dense and denser, gathering myself for a big bang. My
universe will be different. There the wordsmith will rule.

Nightly

after Cristina Troufa's Talking to God

Talking to god on the three-a.m. telephone,
without the phone, on hold to a muzak loop
from a tape baked too long on the dash.

On the other end, some heavy breathing,
a shriek that trails lasting tinnitus.
Periodically, I bash the receiver against

the wall, the way convicts do after yelling
into the cellblock payphone. Bad news.
Bad news. Every night, the call must be made,

the same call, a different call. By now, all
merge into one. Usually, I'm querulous.
God hangs up, and I call again, badgering,

that schmo begging to score with no cash,
a creditor demanding repayment of a debt,
an ex with an ever-unspooling litany.

Loud as it is, no one wakes. From my invisible
sound booth, only I see the incoming call,
recognize the number, pick up to a dial tone.

A Modest Proposal

Already the trucks are rumbling the roads,
rebar rattling. The surveyors have been

ribboning the high desert with what looks like
police tape—Do Not Cross! So many already

have, that's the problem. Lowlifes, scum.
Soon they'll be caged for the upright to peer at,

as in a zoo. Social scientists with clipboards
tallying the meth-addicted mothers and their

low-IQ babies, the gang lords and their
underlings, the rapes in which orifices.

Careful where you are that day so you end up
on the right side of the line in the sand.

Once the final bolt slides, the whole state
drops off the map, an island in a sea of disdain.

Letting Bones Speak

I don't ask for much—a little weather,
a little wonder, a brief reprieve.
Like a cicada, I've grown accustomed

to chrysalis, comfortable in my self-made
sepulcher, scorpions outside lifting claws.
In any alleyway, rats are nothing

but the ovation of whatever leaves us
in the end, the cars of the funeral cortege
pulling away. Once we had maps

as full of yearning as a dog waiting
by the window for the departed.
Now, everyone I know has an answer

they can't recall, red tape over the mouth
of the imagined. Let this be permission
to fail, to lose the war we never signed up for.

Let the water drain from the globe,
the tectonic rattle, joining the history
of broken things, clockworks exposed.

I arrange bones to have something to talk to.
They retail lost cities, ruins loud with singing.
I am ready to believe almost anything.

a collaboration with Jeff Whitney

A Tented Space against Wind

after Erin O'Keefe

Angular, my soul lodges
in the bare bars of a jungle gym,
in a storm window set against fence slats.

Its prism refracts
the day's light, a tumblerful
of muddled clouds, of unspilled weather.

My soul unfolds
a tented space against wind.
Inside, I imagine myself invisible.

Curare-tipped, my fletched
soul arcs through leaf shadow
trailing its hunter's prayer, its blood hunger.

Not complex, but a spare
unfolding, my soul adds itself
to its neighbors, extending its lone geometry.

Seeing Where We Are Led

He requests I use the words *phasmid, pheasant,*
and *incunabulum*, trusting me, somehow,
to grasp what links them beyond their original

Greek and Latin cradles, beyond the joy
of lips and tongue in birthing them, the sheer
pleasure at what they are—the phasmid's

camouflage, perfect down to the stick's
knobbed joints, the leaf's brown edges—
the pheasants, silent as held breath,

until startled into a flash of plumes—
the incunabula, still in their first
swaddling, the massy Gutenberg, the

fables of Der Edelstein. Each serves up
proper awe to those with appetite, the marvel
of the unexpected, the well-crafted thing.

In the same conversation, he laments our
son, held hostage to the screen, wanting
to hand him these words as legacy, and

wanting him to care. I see what he means,
the hours lost to gaming, the zig-zagging
body cam, the sound effects of the kill—

and yet, the same screen brought me an array
of walking sticks, a burred Scotsman
flushing a pheasant, Gutenberg's frontispiece.

How tricky to balance the quick and the lasting,
the virtual vastness, thrumming at a touch,
and the fragile tangible, also thrumming,

and to build a proper house for what one finds,
like a Jesuit, laboring over his memory
palace, rooms holding worlds entire,

strung together through story's fine thread,
leading one through the maze, as I
have led you, covertly, gently cradled.

On Falling in Love at 54

The young me could not hear the canvasses
even though they spoke. To that me, then,

they remained mute geometries, tangled skeins,
perverse, like baby babble, or puzzles unwilling

to reassemble. I preferred the realists, images
conforming to titles like clothes to a paper doll,

seams aligning to limb, the whole tabbed on.
Now, surprised as any scientist, I learn

they've been speaking all along, like the newly
recorded dawn chorus, not of birds, but of fish.

All this while, the reefs, too, have been celebrating
day, heralding night. What did we know, lacking

proper focus, the ability to present ourselves
and lean in? How noisy these works are, in fact,

each shape touting its ambition, colors clamoring
like drunken party guests, line and ground pausing,

interrupting. It's as if I'd finally awoken
at the right time and caught the fairies busy

about their houses, the inanimate bustling, no longer
secretive. All day, now, when not at work, I dote,

like a lost twin suddenly reunited, or a prodigal
returned for blessing. The paintings hold back

nothing, as we do with new lovers, stripping ourselves
to deepest darkness, to mania, to see if this will drive

them away. With the bad manners of one
newly smitten or born again, I want everyone

to see what I see. Picturing past groping, I blush.
Now is the time to repair to a private corner,

to a quiet place where we can marvel,
everything only just now real.

Dear Prick, Priapic

Pull me, please, from winter torpor,
        the limp slog, grey-clotted.
Tug me up by the bulb tip,
        reaching deep to root.
Beat the skin of me, your drum,
        tempo the hectic dervish.
Flood me with turgor, upstanding,
        the waving arms of the faithful.
Seed me in long furrows, hanging baskets,
        along the roadside, wherever,
ringed round to bursting, to the final
        O.

Yours,
Earth

Peroration

after "The Bird Has Flown" by Van Renselar

He has abandoned his chair
        for the capital of a sinking pillar.

As any good orator,
        especially the dying, his arms

stretch wide. He enjoins
        the leaping dolphin and the secretive

kraken. A gull gusts
        into colloquy, wings

mirroring his gestures,
        eye to eye on the subject

of winds. Beyond,
        the horizon flat-lines,

but no crash cart comes.
        Only breaker upon breaker

scouring broken shells.
        Ever-attentive, the sky weeps,

tears frequent
        and unfeigned.

Precisely

for Dirk

All roads approach the same precipice.
Even so, life demands you admire the bruise
of jacarandas against a shifting sky.

In Lagos, you learn, criminals face
their executioners on a sun swept beach,
the surf dampening the booming.

Watching one, two, cannot prepare you
for collapse, but still, you witness blood
become sand. Everything you see fits

in your pupils. On your desk, your death
mask sleeps, shrunken and still, weighted
with a large stone. You print proof

after proof of wave and eddy. In one
resides the perfect tension to pull you
across. You have not found it yet.

Painter to the Moon

after Chagall

Reflector of brighter lights, still, I glow,
        pitted by rock fall,

in lone orbit, turning upon myself.
        Ear cocked inward, trusting

momentum to carry me, I paint
        in a palette of blues.

I crown myself with scavenged
        laurels. Grown stiff

in the posture of a supplicant,
        I hold my piece

of the firmament, proceeding by rumor.
        Fixed, yet wheeling. Cautionary.

Refugees

We're all of us fleeing, fear metallic on our tongues,
bundling up what we can salvage and shouldering it
just steps ahead or behind catastrophe.

We know we're forgetting something we'll forever regret,
that there's no returning to before abandonment.

We already feel violation, the entry of strangers
who do not love these rooms, enemies who'll piss
on what we've left.

A child's voice keeps whispering *where are we going?* It may be
inside us. We clutch hard and shush.

We fold and refold a smudged address, trusting foreignness
to shelter us, or follow others, pinpoints of pain leeching
larger, bled pale.

At fences, our fingers curl through the gaps, barbed wire
spooling like toothed lace.

Even our names may go. We'll carry them as long as we can,
wringing memory from each syllable, then surrendering
them along the way.

The Doula Says Push to the Crowning

after Piet Ouborg's Composition, 1946-50

The day growls outside the window,
too early to say if in menace or play.

Within, we fuck, our own growling,
in menace or play, too early to say.

The sun duplicates itself, casting
a shadow, both double and net

should it tumble when it finally
downs. Here, I cast my own net

should I stumble, should the day
trip me up. The shadows refuse

mirroring, mutating limbs. I attend,
a doula of shadows, a herald

of the first cry. Outside, the day
growls. I ready myself. I let it in.

Epilogue

after Frantisek Muzika

Snake and woman
        enchant one another,

she
        morphing from stone,

it
        lifting delicately from dirt,

all between them
        love,

God's bellow in the garden
        forgotten.

About the Author

Devon Balwit writes in Portland, OR. She has six chapbooks out or forthcoming: How the Blessed Travel (Maverick Duck Press); Forms Most Marvelous (dancing girl press); In Front of the Elements (Grey Borders Books), Where You Were Going Never Was (Grey Borders Books); The Bow Must Bear the Brunt (Red Flag Poetry), and Risk Being/Complicated (self-publishedwith the Canadian artist Lorette Luzajic). Her individual poems can be found on-line, in print, and on her FB page.

www.ingramcontent.com/pod-product-compliance
Lightning Source LLC
LaVergne TN
LVHW020100090426
835510LV00040B/2665